the Painted KITCHEN

Table of Contents

I0892508

General Instructions

Paints

The artists use bottled, non-toxic water-based acrylic paints from several different manufacturers. They are available at your local craft store or hobby store, by mail order, or online. If your craft supply source does not have the specific brand listed, just substitute with similar colors from another manufacturer. Acrylic paints dry relatively quickly and clean up with soap and water. In most instances use the paint colors straight from the bottle. However, artists sometimes specify colors that require mixing or thinning with water. A plus symbol (+) between color names in the text indicates the colors should be mixed. Use a palette knife for mixing: start with the lighter color then gradually add the darker to get the desired hue.

Brushes

The brushes are listed by size and style and include brand information. Using the correct brush size and style will help you achieve the desired effect, but if these are not readily available, just substitute with something similar. Brushes vary in price and quality. It's important to take good care of them, so they'll last a long while. Rinse brushes often during use, but don't let them sit in a water container for long periods of time. After use, clean thoroughly with soap and water (or brush cleaner), working the soap into the bristles. Always rinse well. When storing, be sure brushes are dry and positioned flat or with the handles down.

Surfaces

Project surfaces are available from the source listed in the instructions or at your local craft shop, where you'll also find wood, tin, and other surfaces to paint. Adapt the designs to fit practically any surface you like. You might want to give a "painted face lift" to an item you already have at home. Use your imagination to visualize the designs on different surfaces. Since project surfaces vary somewhat in size from piece to piece, it may be necessary to adjust the pattern slightly to fit your surface.

Preparation

Be sure to prepare your surface before applying the design. Individual project instructions may include special methods of preparation.

Wood surfaces: Fill any holes or dents with wood filler. Sand the entire piece with medium-grit sandpaper and remove any dust. Apply a coat of wood sealer and allow to dry thoroughly. Sand again with fine-grit sandpaper and wipe clean.

Tin/metal surfaces: For old tin surfaces, remove any rust using naval jelly. Wash thoroughly with soap and water and allow to dry completely. Rinse with a mix of white vinegar + water (1:1) to remove any oil or residue. Sand the entire piece with fine-grit sandpaper and remove any dust. Apply a coat of primer and dry thoroughly. For new tin surfaces, wash with warm soapy water and rinse thoroughly. Rinse with vinegar and water (2 Tbsp.: 1 cup) and allow to dry. Apply matte spray or sand lightly with fine-grit sandpaper to add "tooth." Wipe free of dust.

Canvas/papier maché surfaces: No preparation is needed for canvas fabric (e.g., banners, floorcloths) or papier maché.

Basecoating

For most projects, apply an overall basecoat or background color. Keep the surface as smooth and even as possible by painting with a large flat brush and applying several light coats rather than a heavy one. It may take 2–3 coats for good coverage. Always let the paint dry between coats and try to paint as smoothly and evenly as possible.

Transferring Patterns

Enlarge the pattern as indicated using a copy machine. Trace it onto transparent tracing paper using a fine-tip, permanent black pen or pencil. Trace as accurately as possible. Be sure any basecoated areas are dry before you begin transferring the pattern or the lines may be difficult to remove later (a hair dryer can speed up the drying time). Tape the pattern to the surface in the desired position, then slip a piece of transfer or graphite paper underneath (graphite side down). Use gray transfer paper for projects with light-colored backgrounds and white transfer paper for dark backgrounds. Trace over the design using a pencil, inkless pen, or small end of a stylus. Apply with light pressure to avoid leaving indentations on the surface and to keep lines light. In some cases you may need to transfer a design in several steps, starting with the main areas of the design then later adding detail lines. When your project is finished, remove tracing lines with a white art eraser or a damp cotton swab.

Finishing

After removing any visible transfer lines, follow the artist's instructions for finishing the project. Use water-based products because they are compatible with the water-based acrylic paints. Be sure to follow the manufacturer's instructions.

Painting Terms

Doubleload: With this technique, load two colors on the brush at once, which allows you to shade and highlight with one stroke. To doubleload, dip one corner of a flat brush in your first color, then dip the other corner in a different color; the two colors should meet in the middle. On your palette stroke the brush back and forth on both sides to blend.

Float/Sideload: This is a common technique used for shading and highlighting. Moisten a flat brush in water and gently blot out the excess moisture on a paper towel. Dip the corner of the brush in a puddle of paint then stroke back and forth in a uniform motion on your palette. The color will bleed across the brush, leaving strong color on one side and fading to plain water on the other side.

Drybrush: For this method of highlighting or adding texture, start with a dry brush and load the color sparingly. Wipe the brush with a clean paper towel, leaving only a little paint on the bristles. Apply the color using short, sweeping strokes.

Stipple/Pounce: Load the brush sparingly and apply color to the surface in an up-and-down tapping motion. This leaves an irregular pattern of color that covers the base color only partially.

General Supplies

You'll find specific materials lists printed alongside the project instructions. Before getting started, you'll also need to gather the following general supplies:

- Disposable palette paper (sold in pads) for laying out paints. Substitute with freezer paper, polystyrene foam meat trays, or plastic lids. An artist's wet palette is useful if you want to keep paints moist for a longer time.
- Water container, glass jar, or commercial brush basin.
- Pencil, ruler, and white art eraser.
- Various grades of sandpaper and lint-free cloth or tack cloth.
- Tracing paper and a fine-tip permanent black pen or pencil.
- Transfer paper (sometimes referred to as graphite paper) and pencil, dry ballpoint pen or stylus. For transferring on dark surfaces, use white transfer paper or white chalk pencil.
- Paint mixing tool: palette knife, or wooden craft stick.
- Paper towels to absorb water from brushes and for general cleanup.

Chinoiserie Tea Box

by Judy Diephouse

The Chinese art of chinoiserie is traditionally done with Gold and Silver Powders. For this project, the palette list will include the powder for each number and also a metallic acrylic paint. You can paint with either the metallic paints or the powders.

Materials

Surface

Wood tea box with hinged top and 8 inside sections, 12" x 9" x 4", item #252-0052, available from *Viking/Stan Brown, Inc.* (see resources, page 56)

Palette

Gold Powders/DecoArt Americana Metallics

#1—Rich Gold/Metallic Splendid Gold
#2—Pale Gold/Metallic Emperor's Gold
#3—Antique Gold/Metallic Venetian Gold
#4—Fire/Metallic Royal Ruby
#5—Copper/Metallic Bronze
#6—Silver/Metallic Shimmering Silver
*Powders are available at art supply stores and from Judy Diephouse (see page 56)

Additional DecoArt Americana Acrylics

Black Plum, Dark Chocolate, Deep Burgundy, Lamp Black, Napa Red

Brushes

Loew-Cornell, Inc.; 6/0, #1, liners (Series 7350); 2, #4, #8, #12 flats (Series 7300); ½" wash (Series 7550)

Additional Supplies

Satin acrylic varnish, white graphite paper, chalk pencil and ruler, ½" tape

Powder

We will be mixing the powder with satin acrylic varnish. Place a dime size pile of powders for each number. As you need to use that number, add a small amount of varnish next to the pile of powder. Do not pour the varnish into the powder. Gradually mix the varnish and powder together to form a paint consistency. Mix a small amount at a time. The varnish dries quickly and you could waste the powders if you premix too much. You may add a touch of water to thin the paint when doing fine lines. Fresh varnish always makes it easier to work with. Once your project is completed, before you varnish the box, you must clean the entire box with a tack cloth. This is to remove any loose powder that has not bonded with the varnish.

Preparation

1. Basecoat the entire box (including bottom and inside) with a mix of Napa Red + Deep Burgundy + Black Plum (1:1:1). Suggestion: Save some of your basecoat mix for any touch ups later. Sand lightly between coats.
2. Using a worn graphite sheet, transfer the patterns on pages 8-9.
3. Tape off around the edge of the top with ½" tape. You may choose to draw on the crosshatching lines on the four sides with your ruler and chalk pencil. The lines are 1" apart.

Painting

Water

1. Using a 6/0 liner, draw a straight line for the horizon line with #1 powder or paint.
2. Pull fine lines of #1 from the shore and occasionally in the water area. Add fine lines of #1 under the swans for their reflection in the water.

Mountains

The mountains are a strong sideload of #3 powder or paint using a #8 flat. The strongest color is along the tracing lines and gradually fading out to the next line. If working with the powder, load the brush with varnish and pick up a sideload of #3.

Ground

1. Wet the ground area with clean varnish using a ½" flat. Pick up a sideload of #4 powder or paint. The strongest color is along the tracing lines and softens out with streaks into the wet varnish.
2. Add a hill of ground for the lady to sit on and to her left of her dress.
3. The small island is two sections of

茶
TAZO
REINCARNATION of TEA
Passion
HERBAL INFUSION
A tantalizing deep red tea made
hibiscus flowers, exotic herbs
and natural tropical flavors.
[caffeine free]
1
filterbag
TAZO
TAZO
THE REINCARNATION of TEA
Zen
GREEN TEA AND
HERBAL INFUSION
An enlightening blend of
the finest green teas and rare
herbs available in this world.
1
filterbag

ground. The strongest color is at the top of the hills and along the shore lines.

Houses and Bridge

1. The walls, support poles, railings, and crosshatching are all done with #1powder or paint using a #1 liner and #4 flat.
2. The roofs are #5 powder or paint.
3. The door is #3 powder or paint.
4. The trim lines are #6 powder or paint using a 6/0 liner.
5. The bridge is lines of #2 using a 6/0 liner.

Pine Trees and Trees by Large House

1. The trunk and branches of the pine trees are fine lines of #2 powder or paint using a 6/0 liner.
2. The trunks and branches of the trees by the house are #3 powder or paint using a #1 liner. Add a touch of Dark Chocolate to the #3 for the branches of the right tree to show up against the mountains.
3. The foliage on the left tree is tiny strokes of #2 powder or paint using a #1 liner; the foliage on the right tree is dashes of #6 powder or paint using a #1 liner.

Lady with Harp

1. Her face and hands are #6 powder or paint using a #2 or #4 flat brush.
2. Her shirt and waist band are # 5 powder or paint.
3. Her coat is #2 powder or paint using a #8 flat.
4. All of the trim on the shirt and coat are #1 powder or paint using #1 liner.
5. The wood of the harp is #3 powder or paint using a #4 flat; the strings are #6 powder or paint using a 6/0 liner.

Swans and Clouds

1. The swans are #6 powder or paint using a #1 liner.
2. The clouds are a sideload float of #6 powder or paint. Keep these soft; do not use much paint.

Flowers

1. The stems are fine lines of #1 powder or paint using a 6/0 liner.
2. The leaves are #3 powder or paint using a #2 flat.
3. The flowers are sideloaded "c" strokes of #6 powder or paint using a #2 flat.
4. The center of the flowers and extra dots are #5 powder or paint using a stylus or the tip of a liner.

Chinese Word for Tea

1. The design is #2 powder or paint using a #1 liner.
2. Outline the top area with a fine line of #2 powder or paint using a 6/0 liner.

Side Designs

1. Crosshatching lines are #1 powder or paint using a 6/0 liner.
2. Center scrolls are a sideload float of #2 powder or paint using a #8 flat.
3. Start the scroll on the top with the brush flat, finishing the scroll on the chisel edge of the brush.
4. The flowers are a sideload of #6 powder or paint using a #4 flat. Outline with a fine line of #6 using a 6/0 liner. The center dots are #5 powder or paint using a stylus or tip of the liner.
5. The leaves are strokes of #3 powder or paint using a #2 flat. Outline and add a center vein stroke with #1 powder or paint using a 6/0 liner.
6. Where the crosshatching lines intersect, the strokes in each section are #2 powder or paint using a #1 liner. The dot in the center is #6 powder or paint using a stylus or the tip of a liner.
7. The flowers and leaves on the sides of the lid are the same. The scroll lines are #2 powder or paint. The filler lines are fine lines of #1 powder or paint.
8. The bottom edge of the box and the top flat edges inside of the box are #2 powder or paint.

Recipe *Judy's Mushroom Soup*

Saute until tender

1 Tbsp. butter
1 Tbsp. olive oil
1 medium onion, chopped fine
1 clove garlic, chopped fine (2 if you love garlic)
Add 1 lb. mushrooms; saute for 5 minutes.

Add

3 Tbsp. tomato paste
3 cups chicken stock
2 Tbsp. sweet vermouth
Salt and pepper to taste
Simmer — do not boil.

Topping

1 loaf baguette French bread, cut into thin slices, lightly buttered and browned under broiler to golden brown

Just before serving the soup, add the mixture of:
4 egg yolks
2 Tbsp. parsley
3 Tbsp. parmesan cheese
Mix well together; add to soup.
Place toasted bread slice in bowl; top with soup.

Shading

1. Using assorted sizes of flats, the shadows are all sideload floats of Dark Chocolate.

Shade as follows:

a) Between the sections of the mountains

b) Between the hills of the ground on the island

c) The path from the house

d) The left side of each roof

e) The left side of the large house

f) Under the roof of all the houses

g) The right side of the door

h) The right and left ends of the bridge

i) The tree trunks

j) Under the houses and trees

k) Under the lady's chin and lower side of the hands

l) Between the sections of the clothes

m) The wood of the harp and where the strings attach to the wood

n) The bottom of the swans

o) The lower corners of the design on the top

Detail Lines

1. Paint all detail lines with a 6/0 liner using Lamp Black. Check pattern for placement.

2. The lady's hair and features are Lamp Black. Add hair lines in her hair with a mix of Black and #6 powder or paint. The comb in her hair is #2 powder or paint.

Finishing

1. Allow the painting to dry thoroughly. Erase any visible tracing lines.

2. Important if using powders: Tack the entire piece to remove any loose powders.

3. Varnish with three coats of your favorite acrylic varnish. Traditionally chinoiserie is finished with a gloss finish.

Enlarge patterns by 200%

Edge of top

Sides of design

Front and back design

Enlarge patterns by 200%

Tracing pattern

Full detail

Autumn Treats Bin

by Sharon Chinn, CDA

When the leaves start to turn, it's time to bring out the candy corn and celebrate the fall season. This delightful bin is surrounded by the sweet little kernels. Mound it with popcorn balls or other goodies for neighborhood trick or treaters. When those are all gone, toss in your sugar pumpkins until it's time to make pie.

Materials

Surface

Wooden storage bin, 11" square, by *Woodline Works Corp.*, (see resources, page 56)

Palette

DecoArt Americana Acrylics: Avocado, Avocado Dip, Blue Grey Mist, Burnt Orange, Burnt Umber, French Grey Blue, Lamp (Ebony) Black, Mustard Seed, Orange Twist, Sand, Warm White

Brushes

Royal & Langnickel: #2, #4, #12 shader (Fusion Series 3150); ¼" angular (Fusion Series 3160); 20/0 liner (Series 3595); #8, #12 short rounds (Royal Sable Series 5005); #18 round (opt.) (Royal Sable Series 5000)

Additional Supplies

Blue painter's tape, white and gray transfer paper, multi-size leaf stencil, 1" triangle stencil, *DecoArt Dura-Clear Varnish* - Matte, *DecoArt Acrylic Sealer/Finisher Spray* – Matte, size .00 black permanent pen (opt.)

Preparation

1. Transfer the pattern (see pages 16-17) starting with just the lines to divide sections of the bin.
2. With blue painter's tape, tape off border at top of storage bin on inside and outside (see photo, page 14). Paint Lamp Black. When dry, remove tape.
3. Apply blue painter's tape to top edge of the bottom section of the box. Paint bottom of box with Sand. When dry, using an old fluffy brush (or a #18 sable round), drybrush over the Sand color with Lamp Black in a horizontal motion. Apply as little or as much as you wish to give this section a worn, distressed look. When dry, remove tape.
4. Apply blue painter's tape to each side of the accent band between the Black and Sand sections. Paint this band with Avocado. When dry, remove tape.
5. Transfer pattern to front of storage bin using white transfer paper for the lettering and gray for the still life design.

Techniques

1. *Basecoating:* Basecoat the design using as large a brush as possible for the area (normally a flat or angular for larger areas and a round for small areas). Apply color as smoothly as possible. Don't worry if the basecoats aren't entirely even. After floating, drybrushing, and detailing, uneven basecoats will not be visible.
2. *Wet-on-wet basecoating:* Using a sable round, pick up your base color and base the middle area of the section you are painting. Work only in as large an area as you can complete while the paint is still wet. Keep a soft edge into the next area you will move into to avoid a hard line. If your paint is too stiff, you can touch your brush in water and work it into the paint to help it move more easily. While wet, pick up your highlighting color on the dirty brush and fill in the highlight area, then pitty-pat back into the mid-value, blending the two colors together where they meet. You should always keep the tip of the brush pointing toward the direction of the color you just added, blending backward into the previous color; this will help keep your blending softer. Repeat in the same manner with your shading color. You can wipe your brush and pick up more of each color as needed. If your paint starts to set up too much and "pills" as you are working, stop and let

Autumn Treats
Candy Corn

it dry completely, then continue where you left off. To get a clean line along edges, work with the tip of the brush toward the edge.

3. *Brush mixing:* Pick up one color and work it into the brush by blending on the palette. Pick up the second color and blend it in the same spot on the palette. If floating, blend the paint into the brush on the palette in the same manner as a normal float.

4. *Floating:* Float shading, highlighting, or accent colors using as large a flat or angular brush as appropriate for the area (the larger the better). Saturate brush with water and touch against a paper towel to remove excess. Pick up color on the corner of the brush, then stroke firmly and repeatedly on the waxed palette to blend the color into the brush. Strong color on one corner should fade to clear water on the opposite corner. Use short strokes to apply along the line to be shaded or highlighted, and then go back over in a continuous stroke to smooth. Too little water in the brush will cause the paint to skip and drag; too much water will cause it to puddle.

5. *Stippling:* Use a Royal Sable short round appropriate in size to the area. Pick up paint on the tip of the brush, and pounce up and down on the palette to distribute the color evenly through the bristles. Apply to the design using the same up and down pouncing motion. Pounce harder for more concentrated color and lighter for fading the color out.

6. *Drybrushing:* Apply over basecoats to highlight, shade, or accent. Use a completely dry sable short round brush to pick up a little of the color and work it in a circular motion on the palette to blend the paint evenly into the brush. Brush off excess color onto a paper towel. Apply to the design area using a light touch, and work in a circular or crosshatching motion to blend the drybrushed color onto the surface. As more paint comes off your brush, it may be necessary to scrub a little harder, but this will help to softly blend the colors.

7. *Strengthening values:* Drybrush or float an area two or three times to achieve the desired level of shading or highlighting. Keep the darkest values in the little triangular areas of the shadows.

8. *Accents:* Once painting is complete, go back and float or drybrush some colors from the palette into the shadows and edges of the design so the colors repeat throughout. This helps to avoid the cookie-cutter, pasted-on look.

Painting

Basecoats

(Apply basecoats using the wet-on-wet method using a sable round. Refer to step photos, page 15.)

1. *Pumpkin:* Base with Burnt Orange, shading left side with Burnt Umber, and highlighting right side with Orange Twist. Base stem with Avocado, highlighting right with Avocado Dip.
2. *Bowl:* Base with Grey Blue Mist, shading on right and left edges and under rim with French Grey Blue and highlighting center with Sand.
3. *Candy corn:* Base with Burnt Orange; highlight with Orange Twist.
4. *Corn:* Base corn kernel area with Orange Twist, shaded at top and bottom with Burnt Orange. Vary the basecoat of the corn husks using Avocado Dip, shading with Avocado, highlighting with Sand, then with Mustard Seed highlighting with Sand.
5. *Bat stick:* Base with Lamp Black.
6. *Large leaf on right:* Base with Burnt

Orange and Avocado.
7. Let basecoats dry, then sand lightly. Transfer any additional pattern details you want.

Shading/Highlighting

1. *Pumpkin:* Float shade stronger shadow on left with Burnt Umber. Float stronger highlight on right with Orange Twist. Drybrush highlight on right side with Orange Twist, then on upper right side with Sand. Float reflected light on lower half of left edge with French Grey Blue. Drybrush brighter highlight on right side of stem with Sand. Float stronger shadow on left side of stem with Burnt Orange.
2. *Bowl:* Drybrush stronger highlight on bowl just to right of center with Warm White. Float stronger shadow on left edge of bowl with Burnt Umber.
3. *Candy corn:* Paint a Mustard Seed stripe across center of each candy corn. When dry, float shade left edge of yellow stripe with Burnt Orange. Float highlight right edge of bottom section of each candy corn with Orange Twist. Float top tip of candy corn with Warm White (this will be translucent, letting just a little of the Burnt Orange show through). On the candy corn to the left of the pumpkin, float a little reflected light on the shadowed side with French Grey Blue.
4. *Corn:* Using a #4 flat brush, stroke in kernels with a mix of Mustard Seed + Warm White. When dry, float shade the left edge of some of the kernels with Burnt Orange and Burnt Umber to create some darker kernels randomly. Place a Warm White dot in the upper right of each kernel and a fine crescent line in the lower left of each kernel to highlight. Float some Burnt Orange in some of the darker shadows of the corn husks.
5. *Bat stick:* Float edges with French Grey Blue to highlight.
6. *Large leaf on right:* Float right edge with Orange Twist to highlight. If needed, darken bottom edge of leaf with a float of Avocado.
7. *Background:* Float shade background along left side and underneath design elements using Burnt Umber.

Details

1. *Leaves:* I used an ivy leaf stencil with varying sizes of leaves. Pounce in

Recipe *Sharon's Hanky Panky (appetizer)*

1 lb. lean ground beef
1 lb. Bob Evans hot sausage
1 tsp. oregano
1 tsp. Worcestershire sauce
½ tsp. pepper
½ tsp. garlic salt
1 lb. Velveeta cheese (cut into chunks)
1–2 loaves of miniature party rye bread

Brown and crumble beef and sausage, then drain. Combine all remaining ingredients and add to meat mixture. Heat until cheese melts. Spread on bread slices. Pop in 350° oven for 5–10 minutes prior to serving.

(If you would like to prepare ahead, after spreading meat mixture on bread slices, place them on a cookie sheet and put in the freezer. Once frozen, store bread slices in plastic bags in freezer until ready to use. Bake at 350° for 20 minutes; serve hot.)

leaves in varying colors using Mustard Seed, Avocado Dip, Burnt Orange, Orange Twist, and Avocado and a sable round. I used two colors for each leaf, softening them together where they meet in the middle.

2. *Outlining:* Outline and detail with Lamp Black using a 20/0 script liner or a #00 black permanent pen.

3. *"Autumn Treats" lettering*: Using a small #2 flat, paint letters with Burnt Orange. Line top and right edges of each letter with Orange Twist.

4. Candy corn: With Warm White, dot top right of each and paint in a fine line down the right side.

5. *Corn:* With a 20/0 script liner, pull vein lines through corn husks. Use Warm White in the lighter areas and Avocado in the darker areas.

6. *Bat stick:* Finely outline bat (just inside edges) with Blue Grey Mist. Also, with Blue Grey Mist, paint in dot eyes, nose, mouth, and fangs.

7. *Bowl:* Paint in "Candy Corn" lettering on bowl rim with a mix of Blue Grey Mist + Warm White. When dry float French Grey Blue around the letters on the bowl rim, then along the left side on each letter. Float a mix of French Grey Blue + Burnt Orange, shading on both sides of the bowl rim, going over the "C" and "N" to set them back into the shadows. Drybrush over highlight area on bowl with Warm White, going over top of the lettering.

step 1

step 2

step 3

step 4

Sides of Box

1. *Leaves:* Stencil leaves along top borders on each side the same as described in Details – Leaves on page 13. Outline and vein leaves using a 20/0 script liner with a mix of Avocado Dip + Warm White.

2. *Candy Corn:* I used a 1" triangle stencil and Warm White for the candy corn shape. When dry, using a ¼" angular, paint a Mustard Seed stripe for the center section, then an Orange Twist stripe for the bottom section of each triangle. Float shade the left edge of the yellow and orange stripes with Burnt Orange. Float shade the left edge of the white tip with Blue Grey Mist. Outline with Black using the 20/0 script liner or .00 permanent pen.

Finishing

1. Review shading, highlights, and accents. Reinforce, if needed. Clean up any edges or details.

2. When using a permanent pen to line details, brushing varnish over it can sometimes have disastrous results because some inks will smear or bleed. To be safe, always set the ink by spraying with one or two light coats of *DecoArt Acrylic Sealer/Finisher.* Let dry, then brush on 2 or 3 coats of *DecoArt DuraClear Matte Varnish* on inside and outside of storage bin.

step 1

step 2

step 3

step 4

Enlarge patterns by 150%

Enlarge patterns by 150%

Kitchen Bouquet

by Lynne Deptula

Breakfast in bed, afternoon tea, or twilight wine spritzers can be even more special when served with a delightful bouquet of colorful pansies. Display this garden inspired tray on a cabinet top or adorn a wall to add a breath of fresh air to your kitchen décor!

Materials

Surface

Wood memory tray with acrylic liner, 16" x 12" (design area 14" x 9¾"), by *Demis Products* available at craft stores

Palette

DecoArt Americana Acrylics: Antique Green, Avocado, Baby Blue, Black Green, Butter, Cherry Red, Citron Green, Deep Burgundy, Deep Periwinkle, Electric Pink, Golden Straw, Lavender, Orange Twist, Orchid, Peach Sherbet, Peony Pink, Pineapple, Royal Purple, Soft Blue, Traditional Raw Sienna, Vivid Violet, Wisteria

Brushes

Loew Cornell, Inc.: ¾" wash (Series 7150); #2 script liner (Series 7050); #8, ½" shaders (Series 7300); #1 liner (Series 7350)

Additional Supplies

Transparent tape, ruler

Preparation

1. The tray was purchased with a white finish. I lightly sanded the surface to provide some 'tooth' for the background wash and painting to come.
2. Tape off a 1½" wide border around the floor of the tray, creating an insert area. Slip/slap Butter and then Soft Blue randomly over the insert area to create a soft background for the floral design. I did not purposely blend the two colors together, but if they do mix it creates an additional soft green color.
3. Using well-worn graphite paper, a tracing paper pattern and a stylus, very lightly transfer only the basic pattern lines onto the tray insert (see pages 22–23).

Painting

Main Leaves

1. Using a ½" shader doubleloaded heavily into Antique Green and Soft Blue, paint the full main leaves as two stroke wiggly heart shaped leaves (see worksheet, page 21).
2. Paint the smaller main leaves as one large wiggly stroke using the same color blended brush.
3. Shade the back curve of each leaf with a soft sideload float of Avocado.
4. Using the #1 liner and thinned Avocado, pull loose vein lines into the main leaves.
5. Highlight overlapping edges of some leaves with a soft sideload float of Soft Blue.

Purple Pansies

1. Using a ½" shader, basecoat all petals with a sheer layer of Deep Periwinkle.
2. Shade the two back petals on the full pansy with a sideload float of Royal Purple and highlight the outside edges with a sideload float of Orchid.
3. Shade the outside edges of the front three full pansy petals and the partial pansies with a heavy sideload float of Lavender. Further deepen the shade areas with touches of Royal Purple.
4. Highlight the back edges of the front three full pansy petals with a sideload float of Wisteria.
5. Casually tint the outside edges of all front pansy petals with touches of Vivid Violet.
6. Using a #1 liner, pull the detail lines

A garden is a friend that you can visit anytime

in the pansy petals with long thin lines of Country Blue, then a shorter layer of Baby Blue. Pull very short lines from the base of the flower petals with Citron Green.
7. Define the center of the full pansy with two small one strokes of Pineapple.

Yellow Pansies

1. Using a ½" shader, basecoat the yellow petals with one sheer layer of Golden Straw.
2. Shade the base of each petal with a sideload float of Traditional Raw Sienna.
3. Using a #1 liner, pull the detail lines in the pansy petals with long thin lines of Deep Burgundy.
4. Refine the center of the pansy with short lines of Citron Green and two small one strokes of Pineapple.
5. Highlight the outside edges of the pansy petals with a strong sideload float of Primary Yellow, further highlighted with touches of Pineapple.
6. Paint the two back petals on the main yellow pansy with one sheer layer of Deep Burgundy. Shade to tuck the petals behind the purple pansy with a strong sideload float of Deep Burgundy.

Pink Pansy

1. Basecoat all petals with sheer Peony Pink.
2. Shade the back petal with a sideload float of Deep Burgundy and highlight the outside curve of this petal with a strong sideload float of Cherry Red.
3. Shade the front two petals with shading lines and a sideload float of Deep Burgundy.
4. Highlight the outside edges of the front two petals with a strong sideload float of Peony Pink, further highlighted with touches of Electric Pink.
5. Using a #1 liner, define the center of the pansy with short lines of Citron Green and two small one strokes of Pineapple.

Orange Pansies

1. Using a ½" shader, basecoat the orange pansy petals with a sheer Peach Sherbet.
2. Shade the base of all petals with a sideload float and thin shading lines of Deep Burgundy.
3. Highlight the outside edges of the pansy petals with a strong sideload float of Orange Twist, further highlighted with touches in a mix of Orange Twist + Pineapple (1:1).
4. Using a #1 liner, define the center of the pansy with short lines of Citron Green and two small one strokes of Pineapple.

Vining, Filler Leaves, Calyxes

1. Using a #1 liner and a thinned mix of Antique Green and Traditional Raw Sienna, pull loose areas of vining from the main design.
2. Using a #8 shader loaded with thinned Avocado, paint groupings of one stroke leaves casually along the vining.
3. Using a #1 liner loaded into Avocado and touched into Black Green, pull loose strokes to form the calyxes on all the partial pansies.

Outline, Lettering, Rim Detail

1. Using a #1 script liner and thinned Soft Blue, outline the insert area.
2. Using a #1 liner and thinned Antique Green, paint the linework lettering around the tray insert.
3. Using a crumpled piece of paper toweling dipped into Butter on one side and Soft Blue on the opposite side, softly stipple the flat rim of the tray to enclose the design area.

Finishing

1. Erase any visible pattern lines.
2. Brush on three layers of your favorite satin acrylic varnish. Let cure 24 hours between layers of varnish and sand lightly after the second layer of varnish.

Recipe *Lynne's Spinach Salad*

2 pkgs. (10 oz.) fresh spinach; washed, dried, and torn into small pieces
4 hard-boiled eggs, chopped
8 strips bacon, fried and crumbled
1 cup shredded Swiss cheese
Croutons, if desired

Dressing:
1 cup oil
5 Tbsp. red wine vinegar
4 Tbsp. sour cream
1½ tsp. dry mustard
2 Tbsp. sugar
coarsely ground pepper
2 tsp. chopped parsley
2 cloves garlic, crushed

Mix dressing at least 6 hours before using. Toss spinach with desired amount of dressing before serving. Top with eggs, bacon, and cheese. Serves 8.

Actual size pattern

at you can
visit anytime

Coffee Time Quartet

by Doxie Keller

Paint up America's favorite brew on this collection of hot little canvases. Flowers, swirls, stripes, dots, and a palette of rich colors combine in perfect harmony for a kitchen accent that will warm your heart.

Materials

Surface

4 canvases, 6" x 6" x 2", available from *Dick Blick* (see resources, page 56) or have your favorite wood man cut them from MDF board

Palette

DecoArt Americana Acrylics: Dark Chocolate, Light Avocado, Olive Green, Primary Red, Traditional Burnt Sienna, Warm White, Yellow Ochre

Brushes

Loew-Cornell, Inc.: ½" or ¾" flat glaze (Series 798); #4, #8, #12 shaders (Series 796); #1 or #2 script liners (Series 800)

Additional Supplies

3" or 4" roller, *DecoArt Faux Glazing Medium, DecoArt Acrylic Sealer/Finisher,* white transfer paper, white chalk pencil from *General Pencil Co.,* Identi-pen black permanent marking pen

Preparation

1. Using a 4" roller, basecoat the canvas surface covering the top and all four sides. Allow to dry.
2. Apply the patterns (see page 27) and basecoat the patches of Yellow Ochre, Dark Chocolate, Olive Green, and Traditional Burnt Sienna as shown in the photo. Allow to dry.
3. Apply the rest of the patterns using white transfer paper.

Techniques

1. Block in color with 1–2 coats of paint. Use a large brush and stay out of water, picking up only paint for an easy, smooth, opaque application. If you must clean your brush, dry it very well on paper towels.
2. To glaze, apply a coat of faux glazing medium over the surface using a large brush. Working quickly, pick up the glaze color and apply it where you want to change the color. I used this technique to apply Primary Red over the patches of Burnt Sienna and the flowers. When glazing a small area such as the flowers, first load your brush with glaze and then color. When the glaze begins to dry, stop. You may want to apply glazing medium and color up to four times. Glazing medium makes every color transparent. You need not worry about applying clean glazing color since it is transparent.

Painting

Note: After transferring the patterns, continue drawing the design onto the four sides of the canvas. Add 2–4 spirals on each side, as desired, to fill in empty spaces.

1. *Cups and mugs:* Base all cups with two coats of Warm White. Coffee is Dark Chocolate glazed with Yellow Ochre. Use the script liner and Warm White for the steam. Outline with Traditional Burnt Sienna in lighter areas.

Detail as follows:

Design #1: Glaze with Yellow Ochre. Stripes are Primary Red and Olive Green. Shade with Burnt Sienna. Dots are Burnt Sienna done with brush handle. Let dry then add a smaller dot of Primary Red over the Burnt Sienna.

Latte Coffee Sugar
Cocoa Mocha Creamer
Cinnamon Latte Cocoa
COFFEE
CAPPUCCINO
Coffee
COFFEE
CAFE
Coffee
5¢

Add Warm White highlights on handle and saucer.

Design #2: Glaze with Yellow Ochre followed by a glaze coat of Burnt Sienna. Stripes are Olive Green and Light Avocado. Highlight with Warm White.

Design #3: Glaze with a coat of Yellow Ochre. Let dry and glaze with a coat of Olive Green. Darken the handles at their base with Burnt Sienna and also at the inside corners of the cup and around the saucer rim and top of cup.

Design #4: Glaze with one or two coats of Olive Green. Allow to dry and glaze with a touch of Light Avocado near the bottom. Checks are Primary Red done with the #8 shader brush. Stripes are Primary Red and Olive Green. Add black Identi-pen outlining, as desired.

2. *Spirals:* Use the script liner and Warm White thinned with water or Light Avocado over the Yellow Ochre patches.

3. *Flowers:* Base in Burnt Sienna. Allow to dry and glaze with Primary Red. Centers are Yellow Ochre and Warm White. Leaves are done with a #4 shader and Olive Green and Light Avocado. Use both colors on your brush. Start with Olive Green on one side. Turn the brush over and pick up Light Avocado on the corner. Blend slightly and apply a one stroke leaf. Another option is to base the leaf with Olive Green and glaze the left side with Light Avocado. Repeat for all leaves. Allow to dry. Outline with the black Identi-pen or with thinned Warm White as shown in the photo.

4. *Stripes:* Use thinned Olive Green and Light Avocado and the script liner for stripes on the Yellow Ochre patches. Use thinned Olive Green on all other patches.

5. *Lettering:* Use Warm White for Design #1 or Warm White outlined with Olive Green or Black for the other designs (see photos).

Finishing

1. Mist or spray with sealer/finisher.
2. No need for framing, just hang and enjoy!

Recipe *Doxie's Cranberry Chicken*

8–10 chicken breasts
1 can whole cranberry sauce
1 pkg. dry onion soup mix
1 large bottle Western (brand name) Dark Red French Salad Dressing (could probably substitute Kraft French or Russian or a mix of both)

Mix cranberries, dressing, and dry soup in a bowl and pour over chicken breasts. Bake about 1 hour in a 350° oven. Serve with rice or cooked noodles on the side (I prefer noodles). Spoon some of the gravy over the noodles and serve the rest in a bowl.

Serve with cheesy carrots (or a bright green vegetable such as peas or fresh broccoli), hot rolls or fresh warm bread, and a leafy green salad. For dessert serve peeled oranges sliced into rings, coffee, and hot tea.

Enlarge patterns by 200%

Time to Eat

by Shara Reiner, CDA

A touch of whimsy will keep everyone smiling in the kitchen, including the cook. Paint these cheery patchwork letters for spelling out our favorite pastime on a wall or archway. It's always a good time to EAT!

Materials

Surface

12" high papier maché "E," "A," and "T" letters from craft store

Palette

DecoArt Americana Acrylics: Antique Rose, Country Red, Deep Burgundy, Foliage Green, French Vanilla, Hauser Dark Green, Hauser Medium Green, Lamp Black, Orange Twist, Purple Cow, Spa Blue, Spice Pink, Tangelo Orange, True Ochre, Warm White

Brushes

Loew-Cornell, Inc.: #10, #12 shaders (Series 7300); #2 liner (Series 7350); ¾" glaze/wash (Series 7550)

Additional Supplies

Permanent black pen, ¼" wood dowel 4" long, drill with ¼" drill bit, *DecoArt Matte Spray, DecoArt DuraClear Satin Varnish,* star and other "woodsies" for flowers and leaves from craft store (see photo)

Painting

Letter E

1. *Top arm:* Basecoat Orange Twist. Cherries are Country Red, shaded with Deep Burgundy and highlighted with Spice Pink. Leaves and stems are Hauser Medium Green, shaded with Hauser Dark Green and highlighted with Foliage Green. Dots are Warm White.
2. *Middle arm:* Basecoat Purple Cow. Lines are Purple Cow + Warm White.
3. *Bottom arm:* Basecoat Foliage Green. Squares are Warm White done with the ¾" flat brush. Add finger dot in center using Spice Pink.
4. *Spine arm:* Basecoat Spa Blue. The circle flower is Tangelo Orange. Stamens are Lamp Black done with the liner; add dots to the outside end of each line. Smaller circle is Country Red with a True Ochre + French Vanilla oval highlight. Stems and leaves are Hauser Medium Green, shaded with Hauser Dark Green and highlighted first with Foliage Green then with a mix of Foliage Green + tad French Vanilla.

Letter A

1. Basecoat Country Red.
2. Add Foliage Green finger dots with a Purple Cow center.
3. The cross arm is Warm White. Paint checks with the #12 shader and Black. Basecoat star and dowel with True Ochre. Add the center spiral with a mix of True Ochre + French Vanilla.

Letter T

1. *Top arm:* Basecoat French Vanilla. Stripes are Antique Rose done with the ¾" wash brush. Shade bottom of each stripe with Deep Burgundy; highlight the top with Spice Pink.
2. *Leg:* Basecoat Spice Pink. For the plaid use a Warm White wash and #10 shader for first vertical then horizontal lines. Let dry. Overstroke the square where the plaid crosses using Warm White.
3. *Heart:* Basecoat Antique Rose. Shade the point with Country Red then Deep Burgundy. Highlight the round parts with Spice Pink then paint the spiral detail lines with Spice Pink + Warm White.

Penwork

Note: Use the pattern as a guide.

1. *Letter E:* Stitch patches together. Add veins in leaves for cherries. Add

EAT

plaid in small round for flower. Stitch around the flower. Add double wiggly squares inside Warm White squares. Add double wiggly lines to outline star.

2. *Letter A:* Stitch patches together. Add radiating lines from center of dots.

3. *Letter T:* Stitch patches together. Add double wiggly lines on each side of stripes.

Finishing

1. Referring to the pattern and photo, glue the heart to the letter T and the flower and leaves to the letter E.
2. Drill a hole in the bottom of the star and top of the letter A. Insert one end of the dowel in the hole of the star and glue to secure. Insert the other end in the letter A and glue.
3. Spray with one coat of matte spray.
4. Finish with several coats of clear satin varnish.

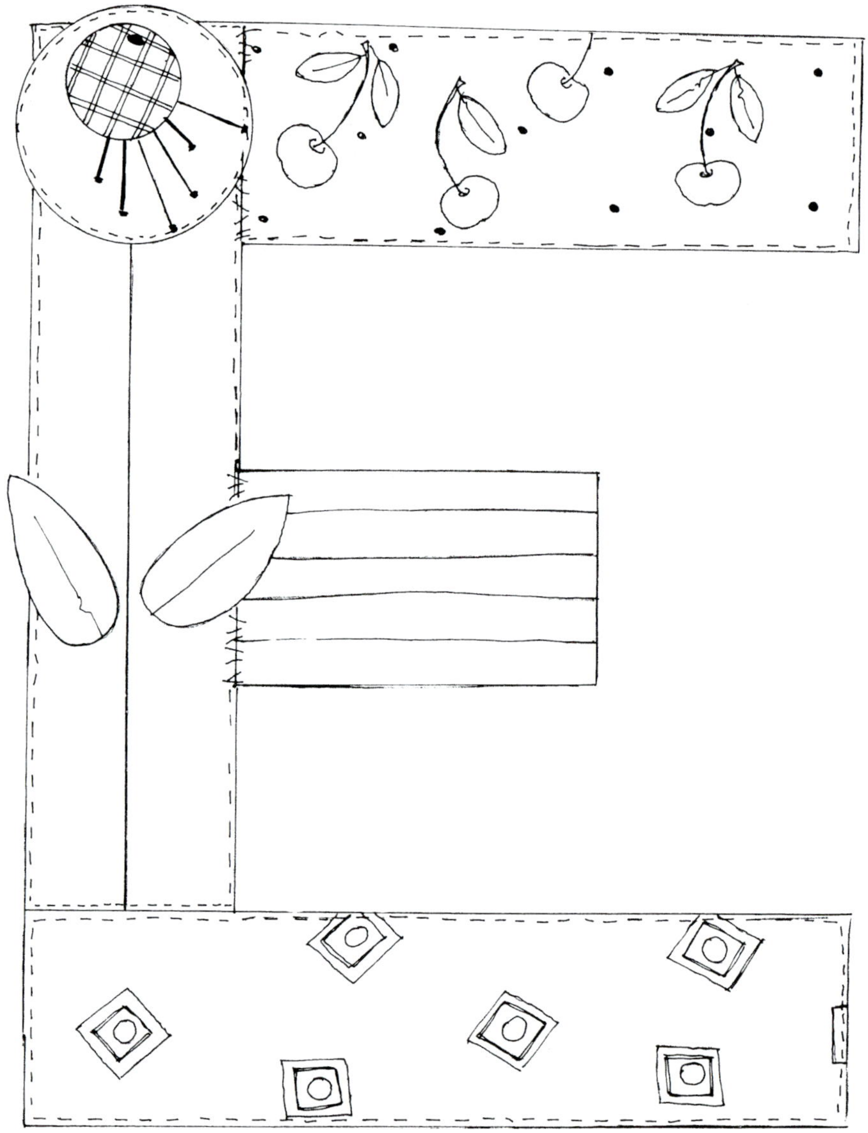

Recipe *Shara's Baked Potato Soup*

4 large baking potatoes
⅔ cup butter
⅔ cup flour
6 cups milk
¾ tsp. salt
½ tsp. pepper
4 green onions, chopped
12 slices bacon, cooked and crumbled
1¼ cups (5 oz.) shredded cheddar cheese
8 oz. sour cream
1 heaping Tbsp. chicken base

1. Wash potatoes and prick several times with a fork. Bake in a preheated 400° oven for 1 hour or until done. Let cool. Cut potatoes into half inch cubes, skin on.
2. Melt butter in a heavy saucepan over low heat. Add flour, stirring until smooth. Cook 1 minute, stirring constantly. Gradually add milk. Cook over medium heat, stirring constantly, until mixture is thick and bubbly.
3. Add potato cubes, salt, pepper, green onion, crumbled bacon, cheddar cheese, and chicken base. Cook until thoroughly heated. Sitr in sour cream. Add extra milk if necessary, for desired thickness. Garnish with additional bacon and cheese if desired.

Yield: 10 cups

Enlarge patterns by 220%

O-o-oh la Latte!

by Lauré Paillex

Coffee, tea or chai? Serve your brunch guests using these fresh linen accessories. The classic earth tones and trendy stripes are the perfect blend of practicality and style. Imagine a gift basket filled with handpainted linens, gourmet coffees, white china mugs, and a loaf of delicious nut bread! O-o-oh la latte!

Materials

Surface

Cotton chef's apron (tan color), matching cotton napkins, and linen dish towel available at local discount department stores

Palette

DecoArt SoSoft® Fabric Paints: Baby Pink, Brown (Dark), Lamp Black, White, *DecoArt Americana Acrylics* with *Fabric Painting Medium* added: Sable Brown

Brushes

Loew-Cornell, Inc.: #1 liner (Series 801 White Nylon); 5/0 fabric detailer (Series 690); #4 round: Series FAB; #4, #8, flats (Series FAB); ½" angular bristle (Series 244)

Additional Supplies

DecoArt Fabric Painting Medium, dry palette, fine-point art pen, painter's tape, decorative fabric ribbon or trim of your choice (I used 8' of 1½" grosgrain ribbon, Sahara Stripe by *Offray* No. RN17991), no-sew iron-on fabric adhesive tape, 2 buttons 1" dia. (to match ribbon)

Preparation

1. It is recommended that fabric items be washed (with no softener), dried, and ironed before painting to remove any commercial sizing that may inhibit the paint from adhering to the fibers. Before applying paint, test a discreet area with a small brushstroke to see how the fabric reacts to the paint. The stroke should hold an edge without spreading.
2. Copy patterns (see pages 35–37) onto tracing paper with a fine-point permanent ink art pen. Arrange traced patterns onto your surfaces as desired, and secure them in place with painter's tape. Transfer the patterns using gray transfer paper and a stylus.

Tips and Techniques

- Iron the fabric to remove wrinkles.
- A piece of Masonite® or smooth, sturdy cardboard covered with plastic wrap sized to fit under your pattern area and held in place with painter's tape will hold the fabric tight and prevent it from buckling while painting.
- A small amount of *DecoArt Fabric Painting Medium* added to *Americana Acrylic* paints will facilitate the movement of the color into the fabric. SoSoft® Fabric Paints do not require additional medium nor do they require heat-setting. Always refer to product instructions on the label. Two coats may be needed for complete even coverage.
- Use a wet-on-wet technique for blending. Add details when basecoats are dry.
- Choose brushes for fabric painting which have stiff nylon or natural bristles. Always select a brush that is the appropriate size and shape for the area being painted.

Painting

Lettering

1. Use Brown for the dark brown lettering. Outline the left and bottom edge of each letter section with Lamp Black.
2. Paint pink letters with Baby Pink. Highlight the middle of each letter section with a stroke of White. Outline the left and bottom edge of each letter section with dark Brown.

O-o-o-h
La latte
café
coffee
chai
tea

Coffee Cup

1. Base the cup with one even coat of White leaving the coffee area inside the cup unpainted. Lay painter's tape along the sides of the cup to maintain straight edges. Use a small flat fabric brush for all other edges, and fill in the main area using a larger bristle brush.
2. Shade the handle and the rim of the cup with a touch of Sable Brown blended into the White basecoat. Lightly brush a vertical shadow to the right of center on the front of the cup. Let dry.
3. Build highlights with White on the rim, handle, sides, and to the left of center. Let dry.
4. Basecoat the coffee with Sable Brown, swirling a generous amount of White into the middle to represent cream. Shade on the left and right edges with Brown. Drybrush the steam with White. Let dry.
5. Transfer the "café" lettering onto the cup and paint with Lamp Black.

Spoon and Coffee Beans

1. Create three distinct gray values—light, medium, and dark—mixing White plus touches of Black.
2. Basecoat the spoon with the light gray mix. While wet, blend the medium gray value along the front edge of the handle and on the shaded areas of the bowl. Let dry.
3. Outline the front edge of the handle and deepen the shading inside the bowl with the dark gray value. Stroke a scroll pattern on the handle, if desired.
4. Add highlights with strokes of White.
5. Basecoat coffee beans with Sable Brown and shade with Brown. When dry, outline and deepen the shading with a mixture of Brown + Black (1:1).

Finishing

1. When dry, any paints which have been mixed with fabric medium may be heat-set on fabric by covering the design area with a clean cotton cloth and pressing with a dry iron. Always refer to the manufacturer's instructions on the product label for complete information.
2. Add a designer's touch to your apron and accessories with decorative ribbon. I chose a tan and pink grosgrain "Sahara Stripe" ribbon by Offray and used iron-on hem tape to adhere the ribbon to the apron bib. (Machine sewing is preferred if item is to be machine washed.) The apron ties are first attached with the hem tape then securely anchored with sewn-on buttons.

Recipe *Lauré's Coffee Date-Nut Bread*

1 cup hot black coffee
8 oz. chopped dates
2¼ cups flour
¾ cup brown sugar (packed)
2 tsp. baking powder
½ tsp. baking soda
½ tsp. salt
1 egg (beaten)
1 cup shredded apple (2 medium, peeled)
½ cup chopped walnuts
2 Tbsp. melted butter

Soak dates in hot coffee and set aside. Combine dry ingredients in large mixing bowl. In a separate bowl, combine egg, apple, walnuts, butter, and coffee-date mixture. Add to dry ingredients and stir until moistened. Pour batter into a greased 9x5x3-inch loaf pan. Bake at 350° for 1 hour or until a wooden pick inserted into the center comes out clean. Cool in pan 10 minutes. Remove from pan and finish cooling on a wire rack. For best flavor and easy cutting, when completely cool, wrap and store bread in refrigerator overnight before serving. It may also be frozen.

Actual size pattern

Actual size pattern

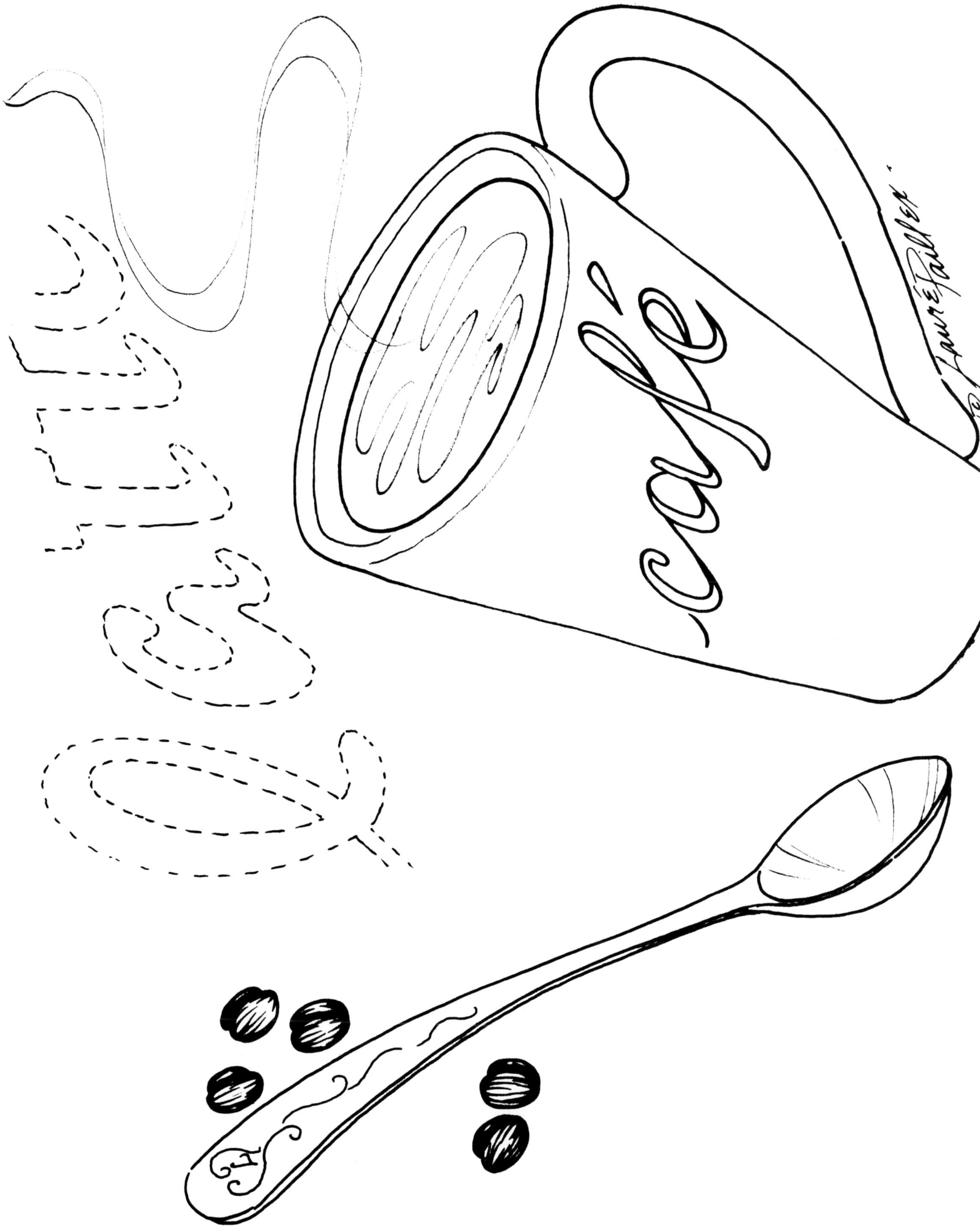
café

Sunflower Keepers

by Chris Thornton-Deason

Sunflowers all in a row will brighten your kitchen with summer sunshine. Stencil a border of red flowers on an inexpensive canister set, then top off each container with one or two big yellow blooms.

Materials

Surface
Sugar, flour, and coffee canisters

Palette
DecoArt Gloss Enamels: Antique Gold" Avocado, Bright Yellow, Burnt Orange, Burnt Sienna, Dark Chocolate, Foliage Green, Honey Brown, Indian Tur-quoise, Napa Red, True Red, White

Brushes
Royal & Langnickel Royal Aqualon: #10 filbert (Series 4170); #12 shader (Series 2150); #1 script liner (Series 2585)

Additional Supplies
Laurie Speltz's Instant Images Floral #IIP01, Laurie Speltz's Instant Images Duo Tool ¼" #IIT07, Delta Creative Stencil Mania Daisies #97 072 0710, low-tack painter's tape, old brush for stippling

Preparation

1. Following the instructions for the gloss enamels, wipe the canisters with alcohol.
2. Apply low-tack painters tape all around the bottom of the canisters about 1½" up.

Painting

Stenciled Background

1. Hold one of the small flowers from the floral stencil in place. Using the ¼" duo tool, pick up a small amount of True Red; pat on the palette to remove excess paint. Using a straight up-and-down motion pat over open areas of flower. Repeat randomly as many times as needed to cover the bottom 1½" of all canisters using different flowers. Tip: Applying two thin coats is preferable; applying too heavily will cause color to bleed under edge of stencil. Use low-tack painter's tape to mask off areas of stencil not in use to keep paint from going through unwanted areas.
2. Using the #1 liner and Napa Red, outline the flowers and dab a few dots in the centers of each flower.
3. Remove tape and use alcohol to carefully wipe the area where the tape had been adhered; allow alcohol to evaporate.
4. Using the #6 shader, band the floral section across the top with True Red. Using the #1 liner band each side of the red with Napa Red.
5. To repeat the red band at the top of the canisters wipe the area with alcohol. Apply low-tack painter's tape around the canisters about ⅜" down from the top edge. Using the #6 shader, paint a True Red band around each cannister. Using the #1 liner, band each side of the red with Napa Red.
6. Transfer sunflower and leaf patterns (see page 42) to all canisters.

Red Daisies

1. Using True Red and the daisies stencil and flower of choice, randomly stencil the flowers around the sunflowers as shown in the photo. Follow the same procedure as for the small flowers from the steps above. Allow to dry. Using the #1 liner, stroke over all of the petals with True Red, Napa Red, or a combination of both.
2. Stipple the centers with Antique

FLOU
SUGAR
COFFEE

Gold using an old fluffy brush; stroke the shadow across the bottom with Burnt Orange using the #10 filbert. Stipple the top with White + a touch of Antique Gold using the old fluffy brush.

Sunflower Leaves

Note: When basecoating try not to cross the colors of one section into the colors of another section as gloss paints are more transparent than acrylics and could take several coats to cover each other.

1. Basecoat the leaves with a mix of equal parts Avocado + Foliage Green using the #12 shader.
2. Using the same brush, stroke the shadows across the bottom and through the center of the leaves with Avocado Green (see worksheet, page 41).
3. Stroke the highlights across the tops and through the center of the leaves with Foliage Green.
4. Reinforce the shadows at the base of the leaves with Avocado + a touch of Napa Red. Reinforce the highlights by lightly stroking with Indian Turquoise using the #10 shader.

Sunflowers

1. Stroke all sunflower petals with Antique Gold using the #10 filbert. Start the petal at the center of the flower pulling out and twisting up on the edge of the brush at the tip of the petal. Stroke a thin layer of Bright Yellow over the Antique Gold.
2. Starting at the center of the flower, pull out towards the tip with Burnt Orange, going about halfway up the petal.
3. Stroke the highlights using the #10 filbert with a mix of equal parts White + Bright Yellow. Reinforce the shadows with Burnt Sienna using the same brush.
4. Reinforce the highlights on the upper petals with White using the #10 filbert.
5. Basecoat the centers with Honey Brown using the #12 shader. Stroke the shadows with a mix of equal parts Burnt Sienna + Dark Chocolate using the same brush.
6. Stipple the highlights by picking up a little Honey Brown, Antique Gold, and White on the old fluffy brush; pat on palette to lightly blend colors and then on center.

Finishing

1. Follow the paint manufacturer's instructions for finishing and cleaning.

Recipe *Chris' Dill Pickle Pinwheels*

1 pkg. thinly sliced deli ham
1 jar baby kosher dill pickles
4 oz. softened or whipped cream cheese

Place a slice of thinly sliced deli ham on wax paper. Spread with softened cream cheese or whipped cream cheese. Lay on another piece of ham and spread again with cream cheese. Place kosher baby dill pickles along one side and roll. Slice into little pinwheels of desired thickness.

step 1

step 2

step 3

step 4

step 1 *step 2* *step 3* *step 4*

Enlarge patterns by 160%

Enlarge pattern by 140%

A Taste of Italy

by Diane Trierweiler

My travels through Tuscany inspired this wine tote reminiscent of the warm Italian countryside, delicious pastas, and fantastic wines. Paint the scene very loosely and avoid going back to correct things. This will make your painting look more impressionistic.

Materials

Surface

Wooden wine tote, 7½"w x 20"h x 9"d available from *The Tole Bridge* (see artists, page 56)

Palette

DecoArt Americana Acrylics: Antique Gold, Avocado, Burnt Umber, Cadmium Yellow, Country Blue, Evergreen, Georgia Clay, Light Mocha, Napa, Olive Green, Raw Sienna, Victorian Blue, Warm White

Brushes

Loew-Cornell, Inc.: #1, #6, #12 flats (Series 7300); ¾" glazing (Series 798); ⅝" angle (Series 7400)

Diane Trierweiler's Signature Brushes: Angel set (short badger fan, sable rake, and badger stippler), 10/0 striper, ½ petal brush (sable and taklon mix tongue)

Additional Supplies

Blue Chacopaper, J.W. etc. White Lightning, J.W. etc. Wood Filler, J.W. etc. Satin Polyurethane Varnish

Preparation

1. Use wood filler to fill in any imperfections in the wood. Seal the wood with White Lightning.
2. Basecoat the inside of the tote using the glazing brush and Light Mocha. Scumble the rest of the surface with Light Mocha and Antique Gold.
3. Lightly sand again and apply your basic pattern lines using Blue Chacopaper (see page 43 for pattern).

Techniques

1. To scumble is to slip/slap two or more colors together in a crisscross fashion. This will give you texture and mottle the color.
2. Tinting is watered down paint that is placed in an area to accent it. Just use a little.
3. Back light means to add highlights into the shadows by adding a lavender or blue color.
4. Wet-on-wet means to apply wet paint into another color or ground; when the paint and surface are both wet, paint spreads and bleeding occurs.

Painting

1. *Sky:* Use your ½ petal brush to scumble the sky colors using Victorian Blue and Warm White. The sky should always be a darker value at the top, gradually getting lighter at the horizon line. Use the same brush with Warm White to "fluff" in the clouds. Leave your brush down on the surface and move it in a circular motion. You can do this while the background paint is still wet. When the clouds are dry, tint the sky here and there just above the mountains using Antique Gold and then a little Georgia Clay.
2. *Background hills:* Use your ½ petal brush to paint the hills with a wet-on-wet method. Use Victorian Blue, Country Blue, and touches of Warm White. Let dry, then tint here and there with Antique Gold.
3. *Background trees:* Use Avocado and Warm White and your badger stippler to place the colors. Let dry, then tint with touches of Georgia Clay. Add a little Evergreen at the base of the tree line.
4. *Foreground area:* Use Antique Gold and Light Mocha and your ½ petal

brush with a wet-on-wet technique. Paint around the villa. Use the same brush to wash in shadows with Raw Sienna. Use your short cut badger fan to stipple in the texture on the foreground hills. Paint with a dirty brush loaded with Antique Gold, Avocado and a little Evergreen. Tilt your brush slightly and move back and forth with the brush stippling in the colors. When this is dry, you can add Warm White to Cadmium Yellow and highlight the tops of the hills with this mix.

5. *Trees:* Use the corner of your short cut fan brush to stipple in all of the trees. Begin with Evergreen and then add Avocado, Olive Green, and Antique Gold. When dry, back light the shadow areas with Country Blue and tint the lighter areas with Georgia Clay.

6. *Villa:* Use a small flat brush to base in the light walls with Warm White. Base the shadow walls with Light Mocha and the roofs with Georgia Clay. The chimney is Burnt Umber. Place highlights on the roofs wet-on-wet with Georgia Clay and Cadmium Yellow. This can be done with your rake brush (angel hair). Use your striper brush with Cadmium Yellow to add bright streaks to the highlight area. Use Burnt Umber to wash in a shadow on the dark sides of the roofs. When dry, use Country Blue to back light the shadow. Highlight the chimney with streaks of Light Mocha. Use your striper with Burnt Umber to add a line under the roof lines. Shade under the roof lines with Burnt Umber. Use your #1 flat and add water to Burnt Umber to paint the windows. Shade the left side and bottom of each window with Burnt Umber. Add a little Country Blue for back lights in the shadows. Tint the buildings with Cadmium Yellow.

7. *Villa landscaping:* The small tree on the side of the house has a trunk of Burnt Umber highlighted with Light Mocha. Stipple the tree top and the shrubs in front of the villa with the corner of your short badger fan using Evergreen, Avocado, and Olive. Stipple flowers in the shrubs with Napa. Use a small flat brush and wash a Burnt Umber pathway from the front door outward.

8. *Flower patches:* Use your short badger fan or the badger stippler to place the beds. Begin with Evergreen then add Avocado and Olive. Let dry, then stipple in the flowers with Napa. Wash an Evergreen shadow under the beds and under the cypress trees.

Finishing

1. You can duplicate the same design on the other side of the wine tote, or simply place in some sky and hills.
2. Shade around the bottle holes and outer edges of the front of the tote with Burnt Umber using your ⅝" angle brush. Place an outline of Burnt Umber around the holes with a striper brush.
3. Trim the edges of the tote with Antique Gold.
4. Varnish with at least two coats of polyurethane varnish and enjoy!

Recipe *Diane's Crazy Cake*

3 cups sifted flour
1½ cups sugar
⅔ cup cocoa (unsweetened)
2 tsp. soda
1 tsp. salt
2 cups applesauce
1 cup water
⅔ cup salad oil
2 Tbsp. vinegar
2 tsp. vanilla
Chopped walnuts

Place all ingredients into a large bowl, stir just until moistened. Pour into a greased pan. Bake at 350° for 30–35 minutes. Let cool.

Frosting

2 Tbsp. butter
3 cups confectioner's sugar
2 heaping Tbsp. cocoa
½ tsp. salt
1–2 Tbsp. milk
Chopped walnuts

Place ingredients in medium mixing bowl except milk and walnuts. Beat with an electric mixer adding just enough milk until smooth. Spread over top of cake and sprinkle with chopped nuts.

Recipe for Success

by MaryJo Tuttle

This super-sized recipe box will keep your favorites organized while adding an artistic touch to your kitchen. The green color on the drawers complements the fresh fruit motif on top, but you may want to replace it with a color to match your kitchen. Be sure to add to your collection the favorite recipes contributed by the artists in this book.

Materials

Surface

4-drawer recipe box, 9"h x 15"w x 6"d, item #252-0041 available from *Viking Woodcrafts* (see resources, page 56)

Palette

DecoArt Americana Acrylics: Antique Maroon, Antique Rose, Avocado, Avocado Dip, Blueberry, Burnt Sienna, Country Red, Deep Midnight Blue, Dioxazine Purple, Eggshell, Espresso, Golden Straw, Hauser Dark Green, Honey Brown, Lamp Black, Marigold, Melon, Mississippi Mud, Payne's Grey, Primary Yellow, Royal Purple, Turquoise Blue, Wild Orchid, Hot Shots – Fiery Red

Brushes

Papillon by *The Artist's Club:* 1" glaze wash; #6, #10, #14 shaders; ½", ⅝" angular shaders ; 6/0 script liner; highlighter set; stipple set; fan set
Loew-Cornell, Inc.: ½", ¾" mops (Series Maxine Thomas); Maxine's Foamie

Additional Supplies

J.W. etc. White Lightning, DecoArt DuraClear Varnish – Matte, brown paper bag

Preparation

1. Sand and seal the entire piece using White Lightning.
2. Sand lightly when dry, then basecoat the top and sides of the box and fronts of the drawers with Eggshell.
3. Using Maxine's Foamie brush, paint the edges of the top, bottom, and cross bars of the box, and top edges of the drawers with Hauser Dark Green.
4. Transfer the main pattern lines (see page 51) and basecoat as follows:
Hauser Dark Green — checks and lettering on the drawers
Country Red — watermelon meat, apples
Avocado — watermelon rind, leaves, strawberry bracts
Eggshell — watermelon between meat and rind
Blueberry — blueberries
Royal Purple — grapes
Antique Rose — strawberries
Golden Straw — Pears

Painting

Drawers

1. Shade the top of the top light checks and bottom of the bottom light checks, to the right of each letter, and both sides of each drawer with Mississippi Mud.
2. Splatter the drawers with Espresso.

Watermelon

1. Stipple the meat of the watermelon with Hot Shots – Fiery Red (this will take more than one application—be sure to let it dry between applications).
2. Shade the bottom of the meat and under the seeds with Antique Maroon. Shade the light part between the meat and rind with Avocado where it touches the pear and grapes. Shade the bottom of the rind with Hauser Dark Green and highlight next to the light part with Avocado Dip.
3. The seeds are Lamp Black and have tiny dash highlights of Eggshell.
4. Outline as necessary with Lamp Black.

Apples

1. Shade around the outside and in the stem indent with Antique Maroon. Shade again to deepen where other fruit overlap the apples by adding a touch of Lamp Black to the Antique Maroon on your brush.
2. Drybrush highlights in the upper area on each apple with Marigold, and

Entrees
Snacks
Salads
Desserts

then with Primary Yellow to brighten.
3. The stems are Mississippi Mud, shaded with Lamp Black and highlighted with Eggshell. Shade the base of the leaf and along the vein line with Hauser Dark Green and highlight the tip and other side of the vein line with Avocado Dip.
4. Outline as necessary with Lamp Black.

Strawberries

1. Shade around the berries and under the bracts with Country Red. Highlight the center of the berries with Melon. Shade the bases of the bract leaves with Hauser Dark Green and highlight the tips with Avocado Dip.
2. The seeds are Lamp Black and have dash highlights of Eggshell.
3. Outline as necessary and add vines with Lamp Black.

Blueberries

1. Shade the berries to separate with Deep Midnight Blue. Highlight the centers of the berries with a drybrush of Turquoise Blue.
2. The end details are lined with Lamp Black and highlighted with Eggshell lines.
3. Shade the base of the leaf and along the vein line with Hauser Dark Green and highlight the tip and other side of the vein line with Avocado Dip.
4. Outline as necessary with Lamp Black.

Grapes

1. Shade the grapes to separate with Dioxazine Purple. Deepen the shading where the grapes overlap each other with Payne's Grey.
2. Drybrush highlights in the centers of the grapes with Wild Orchid. Add brighter highlights to the uppermost grapes with Eggshell.
3. The stem is Mississippi Mud, shaded with Lamp Black and highlighted with Eggshell.
4. The vine around the stem is Lamp Black.
5. Outline as necessary with Lamp Black.

Pears

1. Shade the outsides of the pears pulling in slightly about a third of the way with Honey Brown. Shade again on the left side of the pears with Burnt Sienna. Shade the stem indents and blossom end of the right pear with Burnt Sienna.
2. Highlight under the stems and bottom center of the pears with a drybrush of Primary Yellow (this will take a couple applications—be sure to let it dry between applications).
3. The stems are Mississippi Mud, shaded with Lamp Black and highlighted with Eggshell.
4. The blossom end is lines of Mississippi Mud and Lamp Black highlighted with lines of Eggshell.
5. Outline as necessary with Lamp Black.

Finishing

1. Use Mississippi Mud for the background shading around the fruit and around the edges of the top of the box.
2. Deepen the shading here and there around the fruit with Espresso.
3. Splatter the top and sides of the box with Espresso.
4. Finish the piece with several coats of matte varnish. I like to buff between coats with a brown paper bag; it helps to produce a smooth finish.

Recipe *MaryJo's Clam and Bacon Spaghetti Sauce*

6 slices bacon, diced
1 small onion, chopped
1 clove garlic, minced
1 Tbsp. flour
⅓ cup white wine
2 cans minced clams, not drained
Freshly ground pepper
6 oz. spaghetti cooked
½ cup fresh parsley, chopped
Parmesan cheese

In a wide frying pan cook bacon until crisp, lift out, and set aside. Discard all but 2 Tbsp. of the drippings; add the onion and garlic to the pan. Cook until onion is translucent then sprinkle the flour on top and stir in. Add the wine, clams and their juice, and pepper. Cook, stirring until thickened. Place spaghetti in serving dish and toss with the sauce; top with the parsley and bacon. Pass parmesan cheese to sprinkle over individual servings. Serves 4.

Enlarge patterns by 150%

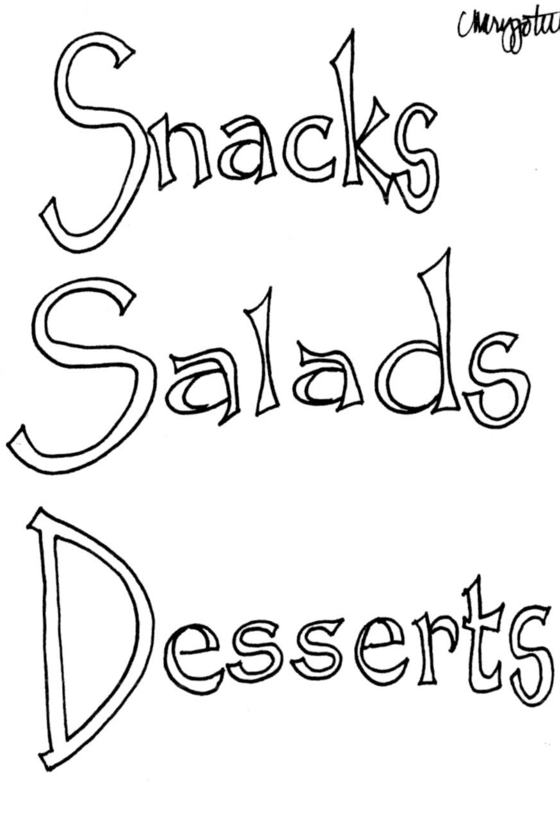

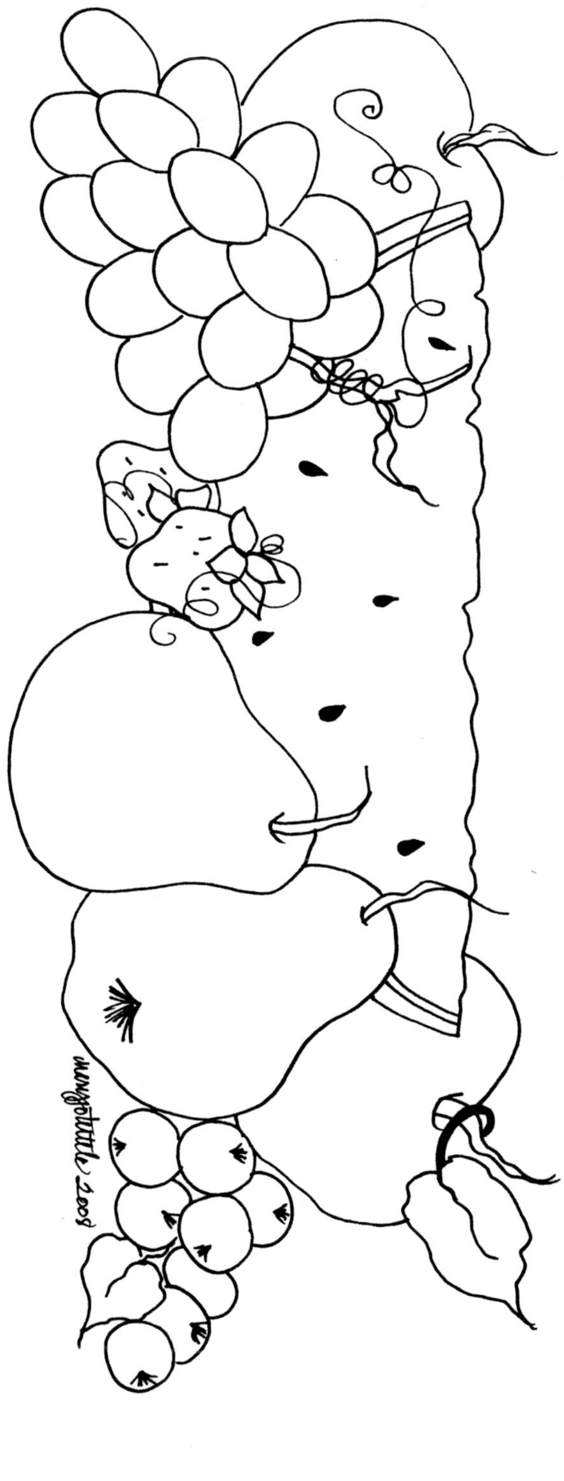

Bon Appétit Chalkboard

by Patricia Rawlinson

A French Country chalkboard will add European flavor to the hub of the house while keeping everyone's messages, meetings, and menus up-to-date. Have fun using wax to create the "chipped" areas for the charming antiqued background.

Materials

Surface

French Country chalk board, 14"w x 20"h, available from www.patriciarawlinson.com (see artists, page 56)

Palette

DecoArt Americana Acrylics: Arbor Green, Asphaltum, Bleached Sand, Burnt Umber, Desert Sand, Graphite, Hauser Light Green, Hauser Medium, Green, Oxblood, Plum, Soft Black, Soft Lilac

Brushes

Royal & Langnickel: #1 oval wash (Royal Aqualon Series #2950); # 8, #12 shaders (Fusion Series R3150-12); ½" angular (Royal Majestic Series 4160); #1 liner (Fusion Series R3595-1); #6 filbert (Fusion Series 3170)

Additional Supplies

Orange cleaner/degreaser, *Clapham's Beeswax Salad Bowl* Finish (available from *Viking Woodcrafts*) Italian palette knife, blow dryer, *J.W. etc. Undercover Black Opaque Primer,* knobs of your choice, 4" foam roller

Preparation

1. To make the chalkboard area, roll on several coats of Black opaque primer; this gives an excellent chalkboard finish.
2. Base the areas where you will want the paint to "chip" with Asphaltum (refer to photo). Apply irregular "chips" of the beeswax (thickly) where desired and base over this and the background with a mix of Desert Sand and Bleached Sand. Allow the paint to dry, heat the chips with a blow dryer and wipe off the wax, taking the paint with it. When all the wax is off, spray the surface with an orange cleaner that degreases and wipe off the waxy residue. Test to make sure you removed the wax by brushing some water on the surface. (If it beads up, you still have wax to remove.)
3. Shade or antique the edges with Asphaltum and spatter with thinned Asphaltum.
4. Transfer the pattern (see page 55).

Painting

Background

1. *Ground:* Wash with Asphaltum.
2. *House:* Wash the roof with a mix of Oxblood + Soft Lilac. Add shingles with Oxblood. Wash the house with Bleached Sand + Asphaltum; shade with Asphaltum. The windows are Asphaltum + Oxblood + Soft Lilac. The shrubs by the house are Arbor Green + Asphaltum mixed with water to make a wash.
3. *Fence:* Paint with Bleached Sand + Asphaltum; highlight with Bleached Sand.

Barrel and Vineyard

1. Base the barrel with Burnt Umber; shade the top with Soft Black.
2. Shade "imaginary" staves with Soft Black; streak this on to indicate staves. Drybrush/streak the stave texture with Desert Sand + Burnt Umber.
3. The bands are Soft Lilac + Asphaltum. Highlight with Soft Lilac; shade with Graphite.
4. The Chianti bottle is Bleached Sand + Asphaltum. Highlight with Bleached Sand. Add details with Asphaltum. Wash the glass of the bottle with Hauser Medium Green; shade with Hauser Dark Green. Add wine to the glasses with Plum. Shade the glasses with Bleached Sand. The sparkle on the bottle and the glass is strong Bleached Sand. The cork is Bleached

Bon Appetit
Bon Jour!

Sand + Asphaltum, shaded with Asphaltum. The ties are Bleached Sand + Asphaltum, shaded with Asphaltum.

5. The grape vines in the foreground are slip/slapped with Plantation Pine and highlighted with Hauser Medium Green. Add grapes with Plum + Asphaltum, highlight with Plum, and repeat highlight with Soft Lilac + Plum. Shade both inside edges of the oval with Burnt Umber.

6. For the vineyard, slip/slap thinned Arbor Green, repeat with Hauser Light Green for highlights, and add grapes with touches of Plum.

Trim and Lettering

1. Paint the trim on the oval with thinned Plum + a touch of Asphaltum. Highlight the edges of the oval with Plum + Soft Lilac.

2. Paint the lettering with the liner and thinned Plum + a touch of Asphaltum.

Recipe *Patricia's Colorful Orzo*

¼ cup olive oil
1 cup orzo
1 stalk celery
1 medium onion
¼ yellow squash
4 cloves garlic
1 Tbsp. chicken stock paste
1½ cups water
¼ green bell pepper
½ carrot

Chop all veggies to a medium fine size; chop garlic but keep it separate. Heat the oil over medium heat and sauté the veggies until the onions are transparent. Remove the veggies from the pan with a slotted spoon. (We want the oil to remain in the pan; add more if needed.) Turn up the heat a bit and toss in the orzo. Toss around in the pan until it turns golden brown. Once brown, toss in the garlic for about 30 seconds. Add the veggies back in and add the water and the chicken stock paste. Cover and reduce heat to a simmer. The pasta will be tender and most of the water should be gone when done. This dish has a creamy consistency without high-calorie cream, and it is delightfully flavorful!

Enlarge pattern by 145%

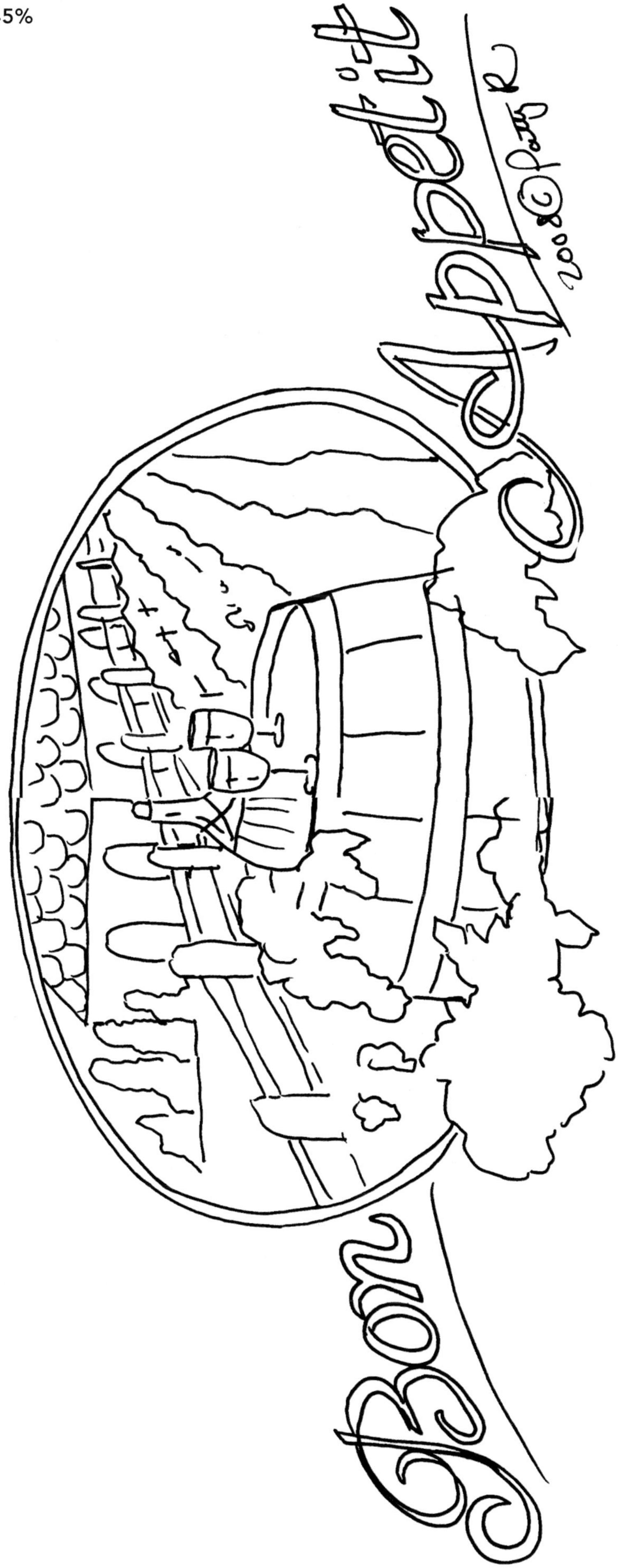

Resources

Artist's Club
13118 N.E. 4th St.
Vancouver, WA, 98684
800-845-6507
www.artistsclub.com

DecoArt Inc.
P.O. Box 386
Stanford, KY 40484
800-477-8478
www.decoart.com

Delta Creative, Inc.
2690 Pellissier Pl.
City of Industry, CA 90601-1507
800-423-4135
www.deltacreative.com

Demis Products, Inc.
PO Box 348
Lithonia, GA 30058
770-482-2600
www.demisproducts.com

Dick Blick Art Materials
P.O. Box 1267
Galesburg, IL 61402-1267
800-828-4548
www.dickblick.com

General Pencil Company, Inc.
PO Box 5311
Redwood City, CA 94063
800-537-0734
www.generalpencil.com

J.W. etc.
1212 N. Tancahua St.
Corpus Christie, TX 78401
361-887-6600
www.jwetc.com

Laurié Speltz
The Creative Coach
8657 Douglas Ave., #130
Des Moines, IA 50322
515-253-9881
www.lauriespeltz.com

Loew-Cornell, Inc.
400 Sylvan Ave.
Englewood Cliffs, NJ 07632
201-836-7070
www.loew-cornell.com

Royal & Langnickel
Royal Brush Manufacturing
6707 Broadway
Merrillville, IN 46410
800-247-2211
www.royalbrush.com

Viking/Stan Brown, Inc.
1317 8th St. SE
Waseca, MN 56093
800-328-0116
www.vikingwoodcrafts.com

Woodline Works Corp.
25 Van Dyke Ave. Bldg. 7
New Brunswick, NJ 08901-3255
732-828-9100

Artists

Sharon Chinn, CDA
726 Meadowview Drive
Villa Hills, KY 41017
859-630-1627
sharon@sweetpatoodies.com
www.sweetpatoodies.com

Lynne Deptula
Distinctive Brushstrokes
7245 Cascade Woods Dr. SE
Grand Rapids, MI 49546
616-940-1899
Dbrush1@aol.com
www.distinctivebrushstrokes.com

Judy Diephouse
Distinctive Brushstrokes
9796 Myers Lake Ave.
Rockford, MI 49341
616-874-1656
distinctj@aol.com
www.distinctivebrushstrokes.com

Doxie Keller
127 West 30th Ave.
Hutchinson, KS 67502
620-665-6256
doxie@southwind.net

Lauré Paillex
P.O. Box 1495
Buzzards Bay, MA 02532-1495
508-579-4623
laureaart@comcast.net
www.laureart.com

Patricia Rawlinson
P.O. Box 938
Gallipolis, OH 45631
503-504-5561
www.patriciarawlinson.com

Shara Reiner, CDA
Angel Thyme Designs
12815 Camino De La Breccia
San Diego, CA 92128
858-395-7588
sharareiner@san.rr.com

Chris Thornton-Deason
P.O. Box 617
Douglass, KS 67039
316-253-5442
cricinda@earthlink.net
www.ChrisThorntonDesigns.com

Diane Trierweiler
The Tole Bridge
1875 Norco Dr.
Norco, CA 92860
951-272-6918
www.dianetrierweiler.com

MaryJo Tuttle
Tuttles Touches
4300 Washington St.
Vancouver, WA 98660
360-693-1938
www.tuttlestouches.com

Produced by:
Kooler Design Studio, Inc.
399 Taylor Blvd., Suite 104
Pleasant Hill, CA 94523
info@koolerdesign.com

Production Team:
- Creative Director: Donna Kooler
- Editor-In-Chief: Judy Swager
- Art Director: Basha Kooler
- Senior Graphic Designer: Ashley Rocha
- Photographer: Dianne Woods

Published by:
Copyright ©2009 by Leisure Arts, Inc., 104 Champs Blvd., STE 100, Maumelle, AR 72113, www.leisurearts.com

We have made every effort to ensure that these instructions are accurate and complete. We cannot, however, be responsible for human error, typographical mistakes or variation in individual work. This publication is protected under federal copyright laws. Reproduction or distribution of this publication or any other Leisure Arts publication, including publications which are out of print, is prohibited unless specifically authorized. This includes, but is not limited to, any form of reproduction or distribution on or through the internet, including posting, scanning, or e-mail transmission.